Best Wishes,

The Song of the Whango-Whee

by John F. Smith
Illustrated by Odette E. Colón
Handlettering by Joey Hannaford

Published by
CHINKY-PO TREE, INC.
Atlanta, Georgia

DEDICATION

To Cappie, who sowed the first seeds of recovery in my heart and mind
and who never doubted this vision.
OEC

To Mary Joe, whose irrepressible enthusiasm for life and graceful spirit
continue to fill me with awe and gratitude. To Christopher and Mary
Margaret, whose great promise humbles and amazes me, may your spirits
always be young.
JH

To Mary, whose soul is as deep as The Whimple Wood and as playful as
the critters who live there.
SP

I live in a hole in the chinky-po tree

Where the limbs
grow big and long,
Where the jack-snap plays
with the bumblebee
And the winds blow
loud and strong.

I drink the drops of the misty dew
That cling to the wish-tish vine,
And I eat the buds of the mystic yew
As I swing on the wild woodbine.

I sing my song to the dreamy moon
    And the stars in the milky way,
I take my rest through the sultry noon
    For I sleep through all the day.

I sleep my sleep in a roly-hole
High up in the chinky-po tree
Where the sunbeams gleam
and the fog mists roll
And the clouds flit merrily.

I make new songs
    as I take my rest
While the woodfolk
    come and go,
And I dream sweet dreams
    in a cozy nest
As I rock my baby-o.